NIGHT PROWLERS!

Curious Kids Press

Bats

There are over 1,200 different bat species on the planet today. In fact, the bat makes up one quarter of all the species of animals. That is a lot of bats! The bat species is broken into two different categories; Megachiroptera (Megabats or large) and Microchiroptera (Microbats or small). People either love them or hate them, but one thing is for sure, the bat is truly fascinating. Let's explore the world of the bat to see what other facts we can dig up.

Where in the World?

Did you know bats are found almost everywhere on Earth? The bat can be anywhere in the world, except the polar regions and extreme desert regions. Fruit bats can be found in the tropical rainforests, where some smaller bats can be found in attics, church steeples, barns and other places.

The Body of a Bat

Did you know bats can range in size from very small to very large? Megabats are the largest. Their wingspan can reach 5.6 feet in length. Microbats are smaller and can be as tiny as a bumblebee. The body of the bat is covered with fur and it has short legs with five toes on each foot.

The Bat's Wings

Did you know the bat's wings are really part of its arm and hands? The wing of the bat is made up of two thin layers of skin. The skin is stretched over its arms and "fingers." Like us, the bat has 4 fingers and a thumb. The skin on the wing runs all along its body and partway down its legs.

The Bat's Senses

Did you know bats are not really blind? Bats can see well in the daytime, but their eyesight is reduced at night. Bats have excellent hearing. Some species of bats have huge ears compared to the rest of their head. Fruit bats use their sense of smell to locate ripe fruit.

The Wintertime Bat

Did you know some bats migrate and others hibernate during the cold winter months? Some species of the bat will journey many miles to warmer climates before winter. This is called, migrating. Other bats will find a cozy cave or other sheltered places to sleep away the winter. This is called, hibernation.

What a Bat Eats

Did you know the bat can eat many different types of foods, even blood? Depending on the species, bats will hunt and eat insects, nectar, fruit, pollen, frogs, fish and blood. The Vampire bat will suck some blood from live mammals such as cattle. Others can eat thousands of flying insects in one night.

The Bat's Special Ability

Did you know the bat uses echolocation to hunt for food at night? This is similar to us shouting and hearing an echo. The bat will make a high-pitched sound. This sound is sent out. When it bounces off of an object, the sound returns to the bat's ears. In this way, the bat can tell where objects are and the distance away it is located.

Bats as Prey

Did you know the bat can be hunted as food?
Some large birds and animals will hunt bats.
Raccoons, opossums, owls and pythons will
catch and eat a bat. Humans have also been
known to hunt this animal. Bats can be
considered a nuisance when in people's homes,
so they may be exterminated.

Bat Talk

Did you know the bat makes sounds? A big part of echolocation is based on sound. Bats can make high-pitched noises that humans cannot hear. This is how they hunt. Other sounds a bat will make are squeaks or clicking noises. Some male bats will sing, display their wings and stand the hair up on their heads to attract a mate.

Mother Bat

Did you know the mother bat only gives birth to one baby at a time? Depending on the species, female bats can carry their young from 40 days to 6 months. The mother bat still has to fly and search for food when she is pregnant. This can be a difficult task.

Baby Bats

Did you know baby bats are called, pups? A baby bat is born without fur. It is blind and its wings are not developed. It will nurse milk from its mother for several weeks. The baby bat clings to its mother's belly for warmth and protection. A baby bat can be raised with many other baby bats.

Life of a Bat

Did you know some bats can live a very long time? Depending on the species, a bat can live to be from 20 to 40 years-old. Bats play an important role on Earth. They can eat thousands of bugs each night. Pollen-eating bats help plants to grow and blossom. Fruit eating bats spread the seeds of the fruit to grow new fruit trees.

The Spotted Bat

This species of bat is in the Microbat family. It can measure almost 5 inches in length. This animal has very large ears. The ears can each be 1.5 inches long. Its fur is black with 3 white spots on its back. It mainly eats moths and grasshoppers and can be found in Utah, Arizona, California, Colorado and British Columbia, Canada.

The Fruit Bat

This type of bat is considered a Megabat. It is also called, a Flying Fox, in some areas. This bat's face looks like a small fox. It has sharp teeth and a very long tongue - these help it eat the fruit. The largest breed of this bat can grow to be 3.5 pounds, with a wingspan of 5.6 feet.

Coyotes

This animal is in the canine family. The coyote is also known as, the American jackal. This animal is very smart and has learned to live with its habitat loss. The coyote has also been depicted in many Native American, Aboriginal and First Nation's myths and stories. The coyote is usually shown as a cunning and clever animal. If you think this is interesting, check out some cool facts on the coyote. Read on to discover more...

Where in the World?

Did you know the coyote can be found as far north as Alaska? The coyote has made its range all over the world. It can be found throughout North and Central America, from Panama and throughout Mexico. It can also be found in many places in the United States and Canada.

The Body of a Coyote

Did you know the coyote looks similar to some dog species? This animal has a pointed snout, a flat forehead and pointed ears. It can measure up to 37 inches long for males and weigh up to 50 pounds. It can reach heights of 20 inches at the shoulder. Females will be slightly smaller.

The Coyote's Coat

Did you know this mammal has a thick coat? The fur of a coyote is grizzled in appearance. It can be anywhere from greyish-brown to reddish-brown. This animal has a thick undercoat to keep it warm in the winter. The coyote has been heavily hunted for its pelt for use in human clothing.

What a Coyote Eats

Did you know the coyote is considered an, opportunistic feeder?   This means the coyote will eat what it can, when it can - even if the prey is already dead. The main diet of this species of animal includes small mammals, fish, fruit, insects, livestock and even larger animals like deer.

The Coyote's Special Ability

Did you know the coyote can run very fast? This animal can reach speeds of up to 40 miles-per-hour for short distances. This makes it one of the fastest land animals in North America. The coyote's own territory can range from a few miles up to 62 square miles.

The Coyote's Senses

Did you know this animal has a strong sense of smell and hearing? The nose and ears of a coyote is its most important sense. This animal can detect hunters and other predators from miles away. The coyote can even hear a small rodent scurrying under the snow.

The Coyote as a Predator

Did you know the coyote stalks its prey? The coyote will hunt small prey from up to 164 feet away. When it is ready, the coyote will make a quick dash or a hard pounce onto its live food. This animal will also hunt as a pack to take down larger game.

The Helpful Hunter

Did you know coyotes are helpful in keeping the rodent population down? In some areas, the coyote is welcomed as it keeps the pesky rodent population under control. This animal has also been known to help out the American badger. The coyote sniffs out an animal in its burrow and the badger runs into it and chases the animal out.

The Coyote as Prey

Did you know this animal is hunted by other animals? Even though the coyote is usually safe in its pack, some animals will hunt the very young, weak or old coyote. These include the mountain lion, bears and wolves. Man has hunted the coyote for its pelt and also because they view it as a nuisance animal.

Coyote Talk

Did you know this mammal can make lots of sounds? The calls of the coyote can range from yips, yelps, barks and even howling. These can be long drawn-out calls or short notes.   The coyote is most likely to make sounds in the early evening and at night or during the mating season

The Coyote Mom

Did you know the mother coyote makes a den for her babies? The female coyote will get pregnant between January and March of each year. She can have up to 19 pups! But the average is only six. The pups will nurse milk from their mother until they are old enough to eat meat.

The Coyote Baby

Do you know the baby coyote is called, a pup? The coyote pup only weighs about 0.5 of a pound when it is born. Its eyes are closed and its ears are floppy. After 3 weeks the pup will leave the den for short exploring sessions. By 12 weeks-old, the pup is learning the skills it will need to hunt.

Coyotes at Play

Did you know coyotes will chase and play with each other? Like dogs, coyotes will engage in play fights, running and wrestling with each other. Coyotes can also wag their tails. This is done when greeting another coyote. This animal's tail will rotate in a circular motion or in a slow back-and-forth motion.

Life of a Coyote

Did you know coyotes can live up to 18 years in captivity? Since coyotes are hunted by man and other animals, so many do not make it to adulthood. If a coyote is healthy and left alone by predators, it could live to be 10 years-old in the wild. Coyotes that live in and around rural areas, run the risk of being hit by a car, or killed by man.

The Raccoon

The raccoon, or sometimes called, a coon, is the largest species in the procyonid family. Some native peoples call this animal, ahrah-koon-em. This means, "one who rubs, scrubs and scratches with its hands." The first known species of the raccoon lived about 25 million years-ago in Europe. There are 4 sub-species of the raccoon. However, they all look very similar to each other. Let's dig into more fun facts about the raccoon to explore its world.

Where in the World?

Did you know the raccoon is a very common animal? This animal can be found throughout North America. It prefers areas with lots of trees and near a water source. This can include mountainous regions, marshlands and even urban areas. In fact, the raccoon can be considered a pest in some neighborhoods.

The Body of a Raccoon

Did you know the raccoon can measure up to 28 inches long? An adult male raccoon can weigh up to 20 pounds. This animal is probably most recognized by its black facial "mask." It has a medium-length tail with black rings around it. It has shorter legs and 4 paws with claws on each one.

The Raccoon's Fur

Did you know the raccoon's fur is very thick? The coat on the raccoon has a dense undercoat and longer top hairs. It is mostly greyish in color with some black intermixed. Its coat keeps it well insulated and warm in the cold winter months. Raccoons also have a slight musky scent.

The Raccoon's Hands

Did you know the raccoon uses its front paws like hands? The front paws of the raccoon have 4 long fingers and a thumb-like digit. This animal can pick up objects with its hands. The raccoon has a very strong sense of touch and will use its paws to identify things.

What the Raccoon Eats

Did you know the raccoon is an omnivore? This means the raccoon will eat both meat and plant matter. In fact, the raccoon will eat most anything from insects, fruit, nuts, acorns, bird eggs and even people's garbage. This species is very good at opening lids of garbage cans and raiding bird feeders.

The Raccoon's Special

Did you know the raccoon douses? This is when the raccoon will pick up its food and appear to be washing it. When near a water source, the raccoon fishes food out of the water and will turn it over in its hands. Since its paws are so sensitive, this is partly how the raccoon tests its food.

Raccoons at Rest

Did you know this animal is mostly active at night? This is called being, nocturnal. The raccoon will spend the daytime hours resting in trees or in rocky locations. Sometimes, a raccoon in an urban area may take up residence in or under people's sheds or decks. The raccoon has also been found in attics and in barns.

Racoons at Play

Did you know raccoons engage in playful behaviour? The baby raccoons will venture out of the den and play with each other. They will run, chase, tumble and nip at one another. It is through play that baby raccoons learn to forage for food and to use their little hands.

The Raccoon as Prey

Did you know the raccoon is hunted by many species? Even though the raccoon will ferociously protect itself by biting and scratching, it does have natural enemies. Large land animals like the bobcat, coyotes, wolves and cougars will all hunt the coon. Man has also hunted this animal for its pelt.

The Raccoon as Predator

Did you know the raccoon will raid bird nests? This species of animal loves the taste of bird and snake eggs. Once it locates a nest of eggs, it will steal them away. The raccoon will also hunt smaller domesticated animals, like kittens and baby chickens. It is best to keep your small pets away from raccoons.

Raccoon Talk

Did you know the raccoon has a variety of calls? This animal can hiss, snort and make a barking sound when it feels afraid. An angry raccoon can growl, snarl and squeal. A baby raccoon will make a squeaking sound when it is being nipped or disciplined by the mother raccoon.

Mom Raccoon

Did you know the female raccoon can have babies when she is only 1 year-old? Mom raccoon will become pregnant between January and March. She will carry her young for about 63 days. She will find a safe place to make a den for her babies. The female raccoon can have between 3 and 6 babies.

Baby Raccoons

Did you know baby raccoons are called, kits or cubs? Baby raccoons are born very tiny - only 2 ounces in weight. They are blind and deaf. They are covered in light fur and their black masks are already showing. The kits are old enough to explore outside the den at 6 weeks of age.

Life of a Raccoon

Did you know most raccoons do not live past 3 years-old in the wild? Due to its many predators and even traffic in urban areas, the raccoon has a short lifespan. However, a healthy raccoon left alone can reach ages of 15 years in the wild. Some in captivity have lived even longer.

Wolves

Wolves are related to dogs. They were the first animal to ever be domesticated (or tamed) by man. This happened over 10,000 years ago. There are around 70 different types of wolves in the world. Wolves have appeared as villains in stories and in myths. Some cultures place high value on the wolf for its qualities. In this article we are going to discover many more cool facts about wolves. So let's get started.

Where in the World?

Did you know wolves can be found all over the world? Wolves have a larger territory than any other animal on the planet. They can be found In North America, Europe and Asia. The wolf will live in forested regions, mountains, plains and even swampy areas. They are highly adaptable!

The Body of a Wolf

Did you know wolves can grow to be around 175 pounds? Wolves have thick coats that protect them from the cold air. Their muzzles are long and they have a broad head with pointy ears that stand straight up. Their eyes are slanted and their tails are long and bushy.

What a Wolf Eats

Did you know wolves are carnivorous? Wolves like to eat meat. The wolf hunts caribou, bison, moose, deer and other mammals big and small. Sometimes if a pack of wolves are starving they will kill and eat the weakest member of the pack. Wolves have also been known to kill domesticated cats and dogs.

The Wolf's Special Ability

Did you know the sense of smell is the wolf's strongest sense? The wolf's nose looks a lot like any dog's nose, but it is highly tuned. The nose of a wolf can smell 12 times better than a dog and 100 times better than we humans. The wolf uses this sense to locate prey and to avoid predators.

The Wolf as a Predator

Did you know wolves hunt as a pack? A pack of wolves will use their powerful noses to track their prey. They always stay upwind, so the prey cannot detect them. Wolves will look for the weakest member of a herd to catch and kill. The wolf takes down its prey from around the neck.

The Wolf as Prey

Did you know that the wolf have no natural enemies except for man? Man has hunted the wolf for its fur and for its tail. Sometimes farmers will kill wolves if they are being a nuisance around their land. This is done to protect the cattle and other farm animals.

Wolf Talk

Did you know that wolves can communicate? Probably the most common sound we hear a wolf make is its howl. Along with the eerie howl, wolves will also yip, whine and growl. Wolves will communicate with each other in the pack. Plus, mom with her pups will make gentle sounds to reassure them.

Mom and Babies

Did you know the mother wolf can give birth to anywhere between 4 to 7 pups? The mother wolf will find a den to have her cubs in. This can be a cave, a hollow log or a burrow along a sand bank. The pups are born blind, deaf and helpless.

Wolves at Rest

Did you know wolves sleep most of the day? Wolves are nocturnal animals. This means they sleep most of the day and are active at night. When the wolves rest, they will find a shady place in the summer and a warm place in the winter. They will all sleep together to stay warm.

Wolves at Play

Did you know wolves like to play? Wolves play much like domesticated dogs do. They will run and chase after each other. They will also play with sticks or branches and practice hunting skills as pups. Wolf pups learn much from playing with each other and by watching the adult wolves.

Life of a Wolf

Did you know wolves are very family orientated? Most wolves live in packs that consist of family members. One male and one female will be the leaders. They are called the "alpha." The weakest wolf will be the last one to eat and is only given the leftovers from a kill. Wolves can live to be around 18 years-old.

The Gray Wolf

The gray wolf is the largest of all the wolves. It is found in remote areas of North Africa, North America and Eurasia. This species looks like a German shepherd or malamute dog. The numbers of this wolf have dropped from 2 million to around 200,000. You can see and hear these wolves in Yellowstone National Park.

The Arabian Wolf

The arabian wolf is the smallest of all the wolf species. It only weighs about 40 pounds. It has short greyish-beige fur and very large ears. Their eyes are yellow with black pupils. This wolf is found in Arabia. Because of the shortage of food, this species only packs during mating season.

The Arctic Wolf

The Arctic wolf lives in Northern Europe, Northern Canada, Alaska and parts of Greenland and Iceland. Its fur is white in color and very thick. This keeps it warm in the sub-zero temperatures. It is medium-size, weighing around 80 pounds. Because of where it lives, the Arctic wolf spends 5 months of the year in total darkness.

Thank you for checking out another addition from Curious Kids Press! Make sure to check out Amazon.com for many other great titles.